Star Pictures

By Leslie Kimmelman

CELEBRATION PRESS
Pearson Learning Group

People can see the stars.

Some people can see
shapes in the stars.

What shape can you see here?

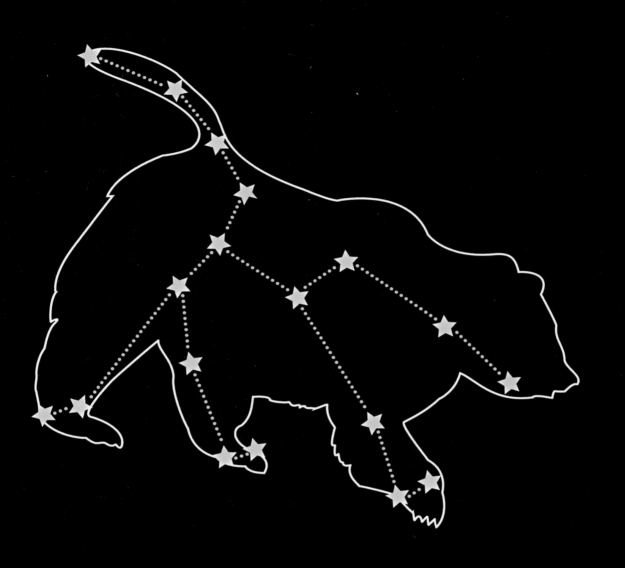

Some people can see a bear.

What shape can you see here?

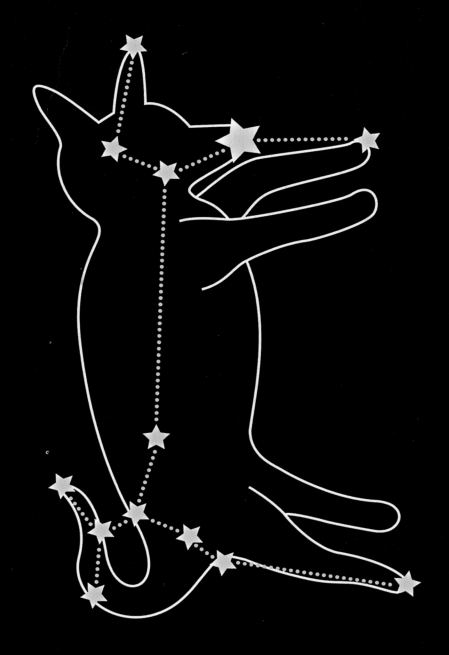

Some people can see a dog.

What star picture can you see?

8